WHEN THE SPIRITS
DANCE

Larry Loyie

WHEN THE SPIRITS
DANCE

LARRY LOYIE
WITH CONSTANCE BRISSENDEN

Theytus Books

Library and Archives Canada Cataloguing in Publication

Loyie, Larry, 1933-

When the spirits dance / Larry Loyie with Constance Brissenden.

For ages 8-13.

ISBN 1-894778-40-5

1. Loyie, Larry, 1933- --Childhood and youth--Juvenile literature.

2. Cree Indians--Alberta--Biography--Juvenile literature. 3. Authors,

Canadian (English)--20th century--Biography--Juvenile literature.

I. Brissenden, Connie, 1947- II. Title.

E99.C88L393 2006   j971.23004'973   C2006-904459-7

Printed and bound in China

On behalf on Theytus Books, we would like to acknowledges the support of the following:
We acknowledge the financial support of the Government of Canada through the Book Publishing Industry Development Program (BPIDP) for our publishing activities.
We acknowledge the support of the Canada Council for the Arts which last year invested $20.0 million in writing and publishing throughout Canada.
Nous remercions de son soutien le Conseil des Arts du Canada, qui a investi 20,0 millions de dollars l'an demier dans les lettres et l'édition à travers le Canada.
We acknowledge the support of the Province of British Columbia through the British Columbia Arts Council.

DEDICATED TO THE VETERANS

The year is 1941, the place northern Alberta,
Canada. Larry Loyie, then known as Lawrence, is
eight years old when his father is caught up in the
Second World War that is raging in Europe.
Many changes come to Lawrence's life…

Papa and Mama and their three eldest children in 1927. This is the only photograph that the author has of his mother. All other photos of her were destroyed in a house fire. Larry Loyie's older sisters and brothers had left home to go to work by the Second World War (1939-1945).

CHAPTER ONE – **On Rabbit Hill**

Night fell slowly over Rabbit Hill. A bright fire warmed the small family gathered around it telling funny stories and laughing. Tall trees circled them like guardians. Overhead the stars were beginning to appear.

Lawrence sat beside Papa, watching carefully as his father put goose grease on the dog harnesses. Papa smiled and said, "This will be your job next time, my son. Make sure you rub the grease well into the leather so it won't dry and crack."

Mama's dark hair was tied back with a moose hide cord. She sat by the firelight, darning Papa's wool socks. Lawrence's mother was a small woman who was always busy doing something for her family.

The family's brown and black dog lay close to older sister Elizabeth. At the sound of footsteps, Buster's head came up. He watched until he saw it was Kokom Bella coming down from her cabin to visit. Little sisters Margaret and Maruk ran to welcome their grandma. As Kokom took her seat, Buster settled his head back down on his paws, quite content.

"A little chill in the air tonight," Uncle Louis said. Their favourite uncle had arrived earlier that day.

It seemed to Lawrence that his uncle knew just about everything. He could read the woods like a teacher reads a book. Uncle Louis knew the ways of wild animals better than most. "It's important to study their habits," he said. "What they eat. Where they rest. Isn't that right, Buster?"

Buster thumped his tail as if to say, "You are right about that."

"That's a smart dog you have, Lawrence," Uncle Louis observed.

"Buster is the smartest dog in the world," Lawrence boasted. "He knows when it's time to pull the toboggan or carry a pack. Then he runs off and hides."

Uncle Louis's laughter boomed into the night. "I had better tell you this in English so Buster won't understand. Tomorrow I'm taking him to my trapline."

Lawrence stared at Papa. "Why is Uncle Louis taking my dog?" he asked.

Papa said, "Food is getting scarce around here because of the war. Your uncle always takes good care of his dogs. Buster will eat well on his trapline."

Maruk had fallen asleep, her head on Mama's lap. "It's time for us to go to bed. Your uncle is leaving early in the morning. He needs to get some sleep," Mama said.

The children followed her into the log house. Long after his sisters were asleep, Lawrence lay awake thinking about Buster.

The bedroom was dark when a creak of the floor woke Lawrence. All winter he had practised listening for the smallest sounds. Now he could hear them even in his sleep. He was proud of his new skill.

Lawrence rose quickly and went outside to the fire.

"You're an early riser," Uncle Louis greeted him.

"I heard you get up," Lawrence said shyly. "I'm getting pretty good at hearing things."

Papa came over carrying a cup of tea. He spoke to Louis in a low voice. "When you use my traps next winter, you have to grease them here. There is no grease up at my cabin. Bears would rip the cabin apart for a taste of goose grease."

Uncle Louis Twin was a skilled Cree woodsman, hunter and trapper. Traditional skills like these were taught to children.

Working dogs like Buster enjoyed pulling sleds and carrying packs.
They also guarded the family against danger.

Lawrence looked at his father with surprise.

How would Papa trap next winter if Uncle Louis used his traps?

Uncle Louis nodded. Swiftly he tied a rope to Buster's collar. "Come on,
you escape artist," he encouraged the dog. "I'll untie you up the hill. You will
like running around in the forest."

With a frown, Lawrence watched Buster trot away. More than anything, he
didn't like being left behind.

A team of two horses. First Nations people took good care of their animals. Horses like Uncle Frank's beautiful black team were used to hunt, gather food and travel. They were an important part of a family.

Lawrence lay on his stomach, his hands under his chin. He was tired of trying to make his toy tractor climb the little hill on his make-believe logging road.

The summer sun warmed his back. He watched Papa's broad shoulders as he carried a heavy log to the woodpile. "My Papa is strong," the boy thought proudly.

A fire burned under Mama's copper boiler. She straightened up from her scrub board and rubbed her back. Her washing was finally done.

"Lawrence," Mama called. "Run down to the highway. When you see a wagon coming, hurry back and tell me. I'm expecting company."

Lawrence hid his tractor under a bush where his sisters couldn't find it. Then he hurried down the trail in his bare feet. Soon he was on the gravel highway. As he waited, he heard the faint sound of iron striking rock. Next came the rattle of a wagon as it bounced on the gravel.

Around the bend came a team of horses pulling a wagon. Lawrence could see the two horses prancing, their necks arched, heads held high. They were the shiniest, blackest horses he had ever seen. The studs in their leather harnesses glittered like silver in the sunlight.

He raced up Rabbit Hill. "They're coming!" he yelled.

Seated on the wagon were his uncles, Frank and Henry. Lawrence loved them both, especially Henry the storyteller.

As he drove the team into the yard, Uncle Frank stood up. "Whoa," he shouted. Keeping a tight rein on the horses, he warned the children, "Don't come too close to Prince and Mistatim. They are nervous today. Wait until they quiet down."

Lawrence

Elizabeth

Uncle Henry jumped down from the wagon. Lawrence stared at him. His uncle looked like a stranger. He wore shiny black boots and a uniform the colour of moss. On his head was a wedge-shaped cap tilted at an angle.

"Tansi," Papa greeted them. "Come in and have some tea." Uncle Henry gave Mama a hug and shook Papa's hand. They went into the house together.

Uncle Frank stayed behind. First he removed the horses' bridles. Next he unhooked their halter ropes. Then he tied the horses to a tree and put out hay for them to eat. Lawrence patted Mistatim's neck as he ate with loud crunching noises. Margaret and Maruk stood back, a little afraid.

When Frank was finished, they followed him inside. Lawrence stood beside Uncle Henry's chair.

"Uncle Henry is dressed funny," Margaret said.

Papa frowned. "Children, behave. Henry is in the army now."

"Will you dress funny, Papa?" asked Maruk.

Mama said sternly, "Your papa is too old to go to war. The army doesn't want a man with so many children."

Margaret

Maruk

Reaching for a piece of bannock, Henry said, "Your husband works hard. He would make a good soldier."

"I will go if I am called up," Papa said quietly.

The men talked until late afternoon. At last, the brothers rose to go.

"Say goodbye to Uncle Henry," Mama told the children. "It will be a long time before you see him again."

Margaret leaned over to Lawrence and whispered, "Maybe we'll never see him again."

"Don't worry, children," Uncle Henry said. "The army is shipping me off to England. I will be fighting in Europe soon. But I will return one day to tell you my stories. Rabbit Hill is my home." He hugged them all.

As they drove away, Henry gave a rousing farewell. "God save the King," he bellowed. "I'll be seeing him soon!"

Lawrence watched the wagon rumble out of sight. The elders always said that it was wrong to fight. Who was Uncle Henry going to fight?

Main Street was a gravel highway in Slave Lake, Alberta, in the 1940s.

The next day, Papa went up the forestry trail to cut wood. The pile of logs grew bigger and bigger. Summer was only half over. Winter was a long time away. Lawrence wondered why they needed so much wood.

Papa stopped to rest and said, "Go with Elizabeth to get the mail. I am going to sharpen the saw while you are gone."

Town was a half hour's walk away. It was built on one side of the gravel highway; the train track was on the other side. The stores and sidewalks were all made of wood. When it rained, mud puddles appeared everywhere on Main Street. Every building had a scraper by the door to take the mud off shoes and boots.

They went straight to the small post office. Lawrence liked the friendly postmaster. His legs were crossed over one another at the knees and he couldn't walk like everyone else. Some people in the town made fun of him.

"I have a letter for your father," the postmaster said seriously. He gave Elizabeth a strange orange envelope.

When they got home, Mama took the envelope, opened it and read it. In a trembling voice, she said to Papa, "Victor, you have been called up."

Their parents went into the house. Lawrence heard Mama's angry voice saying, "Why do you have to go?" Then all was quiet.

At suppertime, the children ate silently. Mama and Papa hardly spoke.

Finally Mama said, "Papa is leaving for the city on the midnight train. The army needs him after all."

Elizabeth started to cry. Soon tears rolled down Lawrence's cheeks. He remembered what Margaret had said about never seeing Uncle Henry again. What about his Papa?

At midnight, Lawrence heard the whistle of the train as it pulled out of town. For the first time in his life, it sounded lonely.

Papa travelled on a Northern Alberta Railway steam train
like the one above when he left for Edmonton, Alberta, for
basic training with the Royal Canadian Artillery.

CHAPTER TWO – **A Mysterious Feeling**

Lawrence knew Rabbit Hill was where he belonged. His father had taught him the names of many plants and the ways of the animals that lived there. Walking alone in the forest that summer studying them, he felt close to Papa.

He loved the trees that towered above him hiding birds and squirrels. Balsam was used for medicine. Birch was used for many things. Thinking about the sweet syrup made from its sap made Lawrence's mouth water.

Tall jack pines grew further up the hill, amid patches of blueberries and low-bush cranberries. Still higher up, near Kokom Bella's house, was a muskeg with a little lake surrounded by tamarack, another medicine tree. It was here Grandma set her rabbit snares. "Rabbit trails are easier to find in the muskeg because they are well beaten down in the carpet of moss," she once told Lawrence.

As the autumn came, Lawrence tried hard not to miss Papa too much. It was easier now that he was in school learning to read and write. Every day he walked with Elizabeth to the one-room schoolhouse crowded with children.

On their way home one fine afternoon, Lawrence saw the first leaf fall. Soon a shower of red and gold descended upon them. "Watch me, Elizabeth," he shouted. He lifted his hands and tried to catch a leaf. It skittered out of his reach. He ran around the clearing, trying to catch just one before it touched the ground.

"I can do it," Elizabeth yelled. She raced from one leaf to another. Soon Margaret and Maruk joined in. Even though she was the smallest, it was Maruk who caught the first leaf. They forgot about Papa and just had fun.

Lawrence and his sister Elizabeth attended the one-room community school in Slave Lake for three years. This photo (top right) was taken the year before Lawrence began school.

Lawrence went outside to the basin of water by the door. As he washed, he listened to the honking geese flying south for winter.

Last night his mother had promised him, "We are having Sunny Boy for breakfast." Even the name of the new cereal sounded tasty. Maybe it was like cake or candy, Lawrence thought hopefully.

Lawrence and his sisters never drank fresh milk anymore. Mama mixed Klim, a white powder, with water to make milk for them to drink.

Food was in short supply because of the war. Mama had a ration book from the government. Inside the book were stamps for milk, sugar, meat, butter, coffee, tea and other things from the store. Mama was careful about her quota of stamps. If she used them up, she couldn't get any more. If she had unused stamps, she traded them for items the family needed.

Sunny Boy cereal was something new. Lawrence hurried inside to try it.

He sat at the kitchen table and looked at the Sunny Boy in his bowl. It was dark brown. He poured milk over it. The milk made from the powder looked blue. He sprinkled a tiny bit of sugar on top.

He tried a spoonful of Sunny Boy. It was gooey and tasted like medicine.

"How do you like it?" Mama asked brightly.

"I like porridge better," Lawrence said. He tried hard not to make a face.

After the first snow fell, Mama put her hand to her heart. "I wonder who is coming to see us," she said. When Mama had that mysterious feeling in her heart, someone always came.

Outside in the yard the snow crunched. A dog barked loudly. "Be still, Flint," a voice commanded.

They heard a knock on the door. "It's Mosoom. Let me in." Mama got up to

Ration book and stamps. Due to rationing, children lived without their favourite foods, notes the Canadian War Museum. Sugar, followed by butter, tea and meat were missed most of all.

let her father in. The children jumped up to hug Grandpa Edward.

"Wait until I warm up," he cautioned them. Grandpa was the oldest person anyone knew but he could still walk thirty miles with his dog Flint to visit. He set his pack on the floor. "It's good to be inside." He moved close to the air tight heater, rubbing his hands together.

"I brought smoked fish for you and the children," Grandpa said to Mama. "With your husband away, I'm sure your family is not getting enough wild meat or fish to eat."

"Elizabeth, bring Mosoom his tea in a cup and saucer," Mama said. She hurried to the stove to prepare something for him to eat.

Grandpa liked to drink his tea hot. He poured some into his saucer and blew on it to cool. He took a long sip and smacked his lips. "Mmmm, wihkasin. That tastes good," he sighed.

After he ate, Grandpa lay on the bear rug using his pack as a pillow. The little girls took turns swinging on his foot until it was bedtime.

When Lawrence got up the next morning, Grandpa was already sawing wood in the yard. Lawrence and Elizabeth helped him pile the blocks of wood. As the morning passed, they talked of many things. They could ask Mosoom just about anything.

At last Grandpa sat on a log to rest. Frost from his breath clung to his face. He wiped the frost away with his handkerchief and smiled at the children.

Mosoom (Grandpa) Edward Twin

"You are both a big help. I am proud of you," he said.

"You are young, Lawrence, but you haul water and saw wood. You work harder than most boys your age."

"Mosoom, am I grown up now?" Lawrence asked softly.

"No, not yet. But you are doing a man's work. Other children have a father at home to look after them."

"Will Papa come home soon?" Lawrence sat closer when he asked.

"I don't know." Grandpa shook his head.

"Can you stay with us for awhile? It's lonely without Papa."

"I wish I could but Kokom Julienne needs me too. She is expecting me home tomorrow."

The next morning, Grandpa and Flint left while it was still dark to get a good start on the long walk home.

Winter passed quickly. Soon only patches of snow were left in the gullies, a sign that spring had arrived.

The sun was setting as Lawrence hurried home through the forest. His mother would smile when he showed her the rabbit he had caught. He was happy to think of her smile.

The evening was filling with shadows. He looked at the position of the sun. "I'll be home before dark," he reassured himself.

Far off in the deep woods something thrashed about. "Think," Papa had taught him. "When animals move at night to feed, they don't make much noise. They are usually afraid of people."

Lawrence walked faster.

"Remember, you are master of what you do in the forest," Papa always said.

The boy slowed down. "Don't panic. Look all around you," he told himself. He felt braver now. "I'm not afraid of anything," he challenged the night.

With Papa gone, Lawrence was always alone in the forest. He didn't even have Buster with him for company. It was all Uncle Louis's fault, he thought.

He was angry with Papa, too. Who was he fighting anyway? No matter how hard Lawrence tried, he couldn't figure out what it meant to go to war. He only knew that Papa was far away, across an ocean bigger than any lake. Would he ever come back to help Mama again? Lawrence's anger made him feel stronger.

In the distance, he saw the welcoming light of home. He hurried the last steps. Mama sat at the table waiting for him.

She took the rabbit with a smile, just as he knew she would. "I'll cook something special for us tomorrow," she said. "We haven't had dumplings with rabbit stew for a long time."

She sat down beside her son. "You are home late. What happened out there?"

Lawrence didn't want to tell her he was afraid. "I heard noises in the bush," he finally admitted.

"It could have been a porcupine. They make a lot of racket when they eat."

Lawrence knew it was not a porcupine. His mother was a good hunter. He knew she didn't believe it either.

"Have something to eat and go to bed," Mama said gently. "You have to go to school in the morning."

Elizabeth and Lawrence ran out of the schoolyard. They hurried past the house that had a mean dog guarding the place. Finally they slowed down.

Soldiers from the United States passed through Lawrence's town on their way to build the Alaska Highway. The first trainload of soldiers (left) arrived at "Mile Zero" in Dawson Creek, British Columbia, in 1942 to start the highway to Fairbanks, Alaska.

"What's seven times six?" Elizabeth asked.

"That's easy. It's 42," said Lawrence.

Elizabeth frowned. "It's not easy for me. I have a hard time with multiplying. But I'm good at reading."

As they neared the railway crossing, they saw a long train standing on the tracks. Young men in beige uniforms leaned out of the windows. Some stood in the doorways of the cars.

"Hey, kids," the men shouted. "Over here!"

Elizabeth and Lawrence stared at the train. They stood alone, too shy to come closer or say anything.

A man yelled, "We're the American army. We're going north to build a highway to Alaska."

An older soldier waved them over. "Don't be afraid. We're from the U.S. of A. My boys are lonely for family, and want to share some treats with you."

Soldiers leaned out as far as they could to hand the children candy, gum and chocolate bars. Some even threw them coins.

All of the soldiers were talking at once. The children didn't know what to answer.

With a few short whistles, the train slowly began to pull out. As it picked up speed, the soldiers cheered goodbye.

"We'll be back!" shouted one.

CHAPTER THREE – **Runaways!**

The postmaster

Hands in his pockets, Lawrence walked along the highway. A lumber truck passed sending gravel flying in the air.

Going for the mail made Lawrence feel grown up. Now that he was at school he didn't need a note from his mother to give to the postmaster.

Two men stood inside the post office. Old Ed, the bottle collector, and Bobby, who hauled freight from the train station, stood talking. They didn't notice Lawrence walk in.

"Nobody left around here but us old guys and cripples," Bobby said to Old Ed. Standing behind his wicket, the postmaster ignored them.

Old Ed's pipe hung from the side of his mouth that still had teeth. "The army even took some of the old guys. Look at Victor with all them kids," he said.

Bobby cut in. "Wasn't Victor in the Great War of 1914?"

Old Ed chomped down hard on his pipe. "That's right. He lied about his age. That's how he got in." Old Ed stopped talking. He jerked his head toward Lawrence. The two men slipped out with their mail.

Lawrence walked up to the wicket. Standing on tiptoes, he could just see above the tall ledge. "Is there any mail for us?" he asked in a shaky voice. He didn't like hearing anyone talk about his Papa.

The postmaster peered down his spectacles at the boy. "Don't listen to those old gossips. They have nothing better to do."

He shuffled through a pile of mail. "I have a letter for your mother. I believe it is from your Papa," he said.

Lawrence took the envelope quickly and hurried to the door. The postmaster called after him, "Hold on, son! Tell your mother to be careful. There are runaways from the army prowling in the area. The police say they are deserters looking to steal anything they can. Some folks have lost food and clothes."

Lawrence ran all the way home. He was panting hard when he thrust the letter into his mother's hand.

"We have a letter from Papa," Mama said joyfully. The children crowded around her. Mama unfolded the letter and read it out loud. Papa missed them very much and hoped to be home soon.

She showed them a postcard of their father wearing his army uniform. Under his photograph were the words, "Somewhere in England."

Papa looked handsome in his uniform. Staring at his father's smiling face, Lawrence forgot all about the runaways.

Mail was scarce during the war. For security reasons, Papa's exact location could not be revealed on his postcard.

The log house was small but it didn't feel crowded. Lawrence and his sisters sat at the table near the wood stove that kept them warm and cozy. After washing the breakfast dishes Mama turned on the radio, her prized possession. Not many families had one. A battery that was big and heavy ran the radio.

Lawrence couldn't believe his luck. The Carter Family was singing his favourite song, "Keep on the Sunny Side of Life." He sang along with them. A beep sounded, marking 10 A.M. "It is time for the news," a man's voice said. Next Lawrence heard, "This is the BBC News coming to you directly from London."

Guns boomed and sirens blared. Struggling to be heard, the man spoke slowly. It was hard to understand what the radio voice said. Lawrence could only make out a few of the words: war, soldiers, battle.

From his mother's sombre face, Lawrence knew the news was not good.

Without warning, Mama jumped up and clicked off the radio. She grabbed her apron and tied it on. "Go play outside, children," she ordered. "I have to scrub the floor."

The girls put on their coats and went outside. Lawrence lingered behind, afraid to ask if Papa was safe.

The family listened to a battery-operated radio like this one.

"Do you want something?" Mama said.

Almost whispering, Lawrence asked, "Is the war going to be over soon?"

"No one knows," Mama said sharply. "Now fetch me a pail of water for my floor."

Lawrence and Elizabeth stood at the top of a steep sandy hill, waiting for Margaret and Maruk to join them.

Kokom (Grandma) Bella Twin in front of her home on Rabbit Hill.

"I'm first!" With a whoop, Lawrence jumped off the ledge and slid down the sand. At the bottom, he clambered out of the way. A second later Margaret landed behind him.

Next it was Maruk's turn. Little sister slipped and rolled down the hill. She looked as if she was going to cry.

"Don't be a baby," Margaret said. She pulled Maruk to her feet.

Scrambling up the hill, Lawrence hurried to the top again.

Suddenly he heard a cry.

"Help, children, help," Mama screamed.

Clutching two bags of groceries, she ran toward them. Lawrence saw a man in a dirty green coat and heavy black boots chasing her, getting closer with every step. His beard was shaggy and his eyes were mean.

The children ran to Mama. Lawrence was the fastest. "Get away from her," he shouted at the man. As Lawrence rushed forward, the stranger ran into the forest and vanished.

Elizabeth and the girls huddled around Mama to protect her. Catching her breath, Mama rested by the road. "I should have known better than to carry so many groceries from town. I sure wasn't going to give them up," she said.

Grandma Bella was waiting for them in their yard. She carried her little rabbit gun under her arm.

"I heard your Mama and came right away," Grandma said. "A runaway tried to break into my place while I was out hunting. It must have been the same man. He left knife marks on my door. Lucky I have a good chain and padlock on it."

After supper, Lawrence and Elizabeth sat in the yard.

"What's wrong?" Elizabeth asked. "You didn't say much at supper."

The words stuck in Lawrence's throat. "The postmaster warned me about the runaways. I forgot to tell Mama. It's all my fault."

"Mama knew about them already," Elizabeth said. "She told me so."

"I still feel bad."

Elizabeth patted his shoulder. "Mama knows we were brave. No one will ever scare us again," she promised.

Her promise made them both feel better.

One morning a few days later, Mama stood at the window. The spring sunshine was bright and inviting. "I see Mother Nature is up to her little tricks," she said with a laugh.

Lawrence looked up from his schoolbook. A long time had passed since he had heard his mother laugh.

Mama said, "I've been watching the birch trees. Children, let us go and test them for sap."

They followed her up the trail. She picked up a stick and used it as a pointer. "See that branch? The buds tell me the sap is ready to make syrup.

The birch trees are waiting for us at our old campsite. We must leave right away to collect the sap."

"Can I camp alone when we're in the bush?" Lawrence surprised himself by asking.

Mama stopped walking and looked at him. "You have been a big help to me, my son. Yes, you can," she replied. "As long as you are close enough so that Kokom and I can see your campfire."

Lawrence thought about Sammy, his cousin. Sammy's father was home all the time, while Papa was far away. It wasn't fair. On the other hand, he could do grown-up things now that Sammy wasn't allowed to do. It would be a long time before his cousin was allowed to camp alone. It made Lawrence feel a little better to know he was outdoing Sammy.

Campsites like this one are used from year-to-year, as long as there is wood nearby for a fire. They were used for drying meat, cooking birch syrup, and as a family gathering place.

CHAPTER FOUR – **When the Spirits Dance**

The birch trees grew tall. Curls of white, tan and brown papery bark fluttered in the breeze.

The old camp was in a small clearing not far from their house. They all had jobs to do. Kokom Bella and the girls collected firewood. Grandma's dog Whiskers ran around their legs, almost tripping Elizabeth.

Lawrence walked into the bush with Mama.

"I'll tap some trees to see how the sap is flowing," she said.

With a small axe, she cut a notch on a tree. Next she hung a bucket below the notch. "Now we must wait for the sap to come to the opening." Together they moved on to more trees.

After a while Mama went back to the first bucket. "The sap is flowing freely," she said. "I will give thanks for the gifts of the birch tree with an offering." From her pocket, she took a handful of tobacco and put it in the earth.

Filling a cup with the fresh sap, Mama gathered the family around her. Each child drank from the cup. The sap was clear and sweet.

"Sap is good medicine, especially for children. When we drink it we honour the tree for giving us its life water," Mama said.

By late afternoon, they had filled a large cauldron with sap. Mama and Grandma hung it on a sturdy hook over the fire, adding more logs beneath it. With a satisfied look, Mama said, "Soon we will have sweet birch syrup."

The family relaxed around the fire. Grandma picked up a curling strip of birch bark and showed it to the children. "When you go into the bush, take a handful of this with you. It makes a fire quickly. Now I have something else to show you."

From under her blanket, Grandma pulled out a moose horn made of birch bark. "I made this moose caller while you were busy working," she said.

"Do moose really come when you call them?" Maruk asked.

"Of course! All we have to do is try it. Who is going to be first?"

As always, Margaret wanted to go first. She blew into the horn and a squeak came out. "That might get us a mouse but not a moose," Grandma joked.

Maruk tried next. She made a noisy squawk. Whiskers got up and went to a new spot under a tree. Mama and Grandma laughed so hard that tears came to their eyes.

Lawrence took the moose horn. His call sounded a bit like a moose but a lot more like a bullfrog.

Now it was Elizabeth's turn. Breathing deeply, she grunted slowly and lightly. Soon the grunts came louder and faster, just like a real moose.

Loud crashes came from the forest. The family stared in amazement. Margaret screeched, "It's a moose. We have to hide."

"That's not possible. But whatever it is sure makes a lot of racket," Mama said.

Just then a man dressed in an old suit ran out of the trees. His pants were torn and he carried his cap. His hair stuck out all over his head.

Mama and Grandma burst out laughing. "Mah! It's only Puya," Grandma exclaimed. "What are you doing scaring my grandchildren?"

Lawrence burst out laughing, too. The moose horn had called his favourite storyteller to their camp.

"Kayas. It's been a long time," Puya greeted the family. Rubbing his stomach, he groaned. "I was all alone when I got hungry. So of course I went out to find some supper. First I saw a deer and chased after it. All of a sudden that deer turned into a rabbit. I said to myself, oh well, a rabbit for my evening

Birch curls with a moose horn of birch bark. A blanket and matches for a fire (below) kept Lawrence warm at night.

meal will do nicely. By this time my legs were so tired I chased that rabbit on all fours. That's why it got away."

He winked at the children. "When I heard your beautiful moose calls, I came right here. I remembered your Grandpa asked me to visit and see how you were doing."

Grandma gave Puya a big bowl of soup and a thick slice of bannock. "You will have to earn your supper. You can help us haul wood for the fire," she teased.

Puya ate his soup with loud slurps. "I'm making this noise because your soup is good," he grinned.

Soon the sun was setting. Elizabeth gathered up Margaret and Maruk to take them home to bed.

"Take Whiskers with you for company," Mama said. "He will bark at anything bigger than an ant. I'll be along as soon as the sap starts to boil."

All day Lawrence thought about camping alone. He rolled his blanket carefully and added matches to light a fire. Now that night was near, he felt uneasy about sleeping alone in the bush.

He remembered Mosoom Edward saying, "You can imagine all kinds of crazy things to stop you from doing what you want to do. The mind is remarkable in that way." He was deep in thought when Grandma called him over.

"You are young to be camping alone. Pick a spot that is sheltered from rain and wind," she said.

Lawrence dug into his pocket. "I have a handful of birch bark to start my fire."

Grandma approved. "Remember the lessons you have learned. Your life may depend on it," she added.

Lawrence set off with his bedroll under his arm.

"He'll be all right," he heard Grandma say.

More confident now, he hummed his favourite tune, "Keep on the Sunny Side of Life."

Before long, he found a sheltered spot under a tall spruce tree and made a little fire to keep the mosquitoes away. One by one, the stars appeared. Studying the sky, he fell asleep.

Soon he dreamed he was in a dark forest. Strange shadows sprung up around him. Tree branches grabbed at him. A cold wind made the spruce trees bow before him.

From behind the waving branches, a giant cougar stalked him. Lawrence spun around to run but the cougar was everywhere. It chased him, swiping at his back with sharp claws.

In his dream, Lawrence saw Papa (Victor Loyie) in his Canadian Armed Forces uniform. He served in the Great War of 1914-1918 (First World War) as well as the Second World War.

Cougar and grizzly bear

Lawrence tried to speak but no sound came out. Terrified, he looked around for help. In the distance he saw his father. "Papa," he cried as he raced toward him. As he got closer, Papa vanished.

Determined to do battle, Lawrence found his pocketknife. From out of nowhere, a grizzly bear appeared. The bear jumped at the cougar, pushing the boy aside to save him. Lawrence fell to the ground as the cougar rushed past. Pain shot up his arm. He moaned and woke up.

Lawrence was grateful to be awake. He felt a little foolish, too. His arm was sore from lying on it in his sleep.

Twigs cracked in the bush. Once. Twice. Lawrence turned toward the sounds. Hidden by the low spruce branches, he peered into the darkness. Squinting his eyes he saw a movement in the forest. It couldn't be an animal, he knew. Animals wouldn't sneak up to a fire.

Silently Lawrence got up. He slipped back to the camp. Mama, Grandma and Puya were sitting quietly together. Startled to see him, Grandma asked, "What's the matter?"

"Someone is out there," Lawrence whispered. He pointed to the dark.

At the edge of the forest, they saw a man creeping toward their supplies. His bushy beard jutted out from his face.

With a shout, Puya grabbed his walking stick. Waving it in the air, he ran toward the stranger. The rough-looking man disappeared like a shadow.

The storyteller stopped and listened for a long time. When he was satisfied, he returned to the fire. "That man is one of the runaways from the army. They seem to be all over the country. The police are patrolling the highway for deserters like him. That is why the runaways travel in the bush. He won't dare come back now."

Mama hugged Lawrence. "Thank goodness you warned us. He could have taken all of our supplies."

Lawrence hesitated. He could still pretend that everything was all right. But if he did, he knew the bad feeling would never go away.

He forced himself to look at his mother. "The postmaster told me about the runaways. I forgot to warn you. I'm sorry," he said.

Mama stared at him. Then she said, "You are right, my son, you should have told me. But it is better to know that you are honest." She hugged him again.

"I'll go home and stay with the girls," Mama said. She hurried off.

Puya put his stick down and smiled at Grandma. "That runaway must be really hungry to come this close. I told you your soup was good," he said.

Grandma put her rabbit gun near the fire. "Just to be on the safe side," she said.

Wrapped in a thick blanket, Puya snored by the fire. "Sit beside me," Grandma said to Lawrence. "You have had enough excitement for one night." She poured him a cup of tea that warmed him nicely inside.

"How did you hear the runaway?" Grandma asked.

"I had a dream. First I saw Papa but he went away. I was going to fight a cougar but a grizzly bear saved me. I woke up and heard a noise."

Grandma stirred the boiling sap. When she spoke, it was in a knowing way. "The grizzly is your spirit animal. You are fortunate to have such a powerful animal to protect you. Dreams are good medicine. They will make you strong."

Lawrence listened thoughtfully. "Will I dream about the grizzly bear again?" he asked.

"Your spirit animal will come when you need it. The grizzly is noble and fears nothing in his territory. You must learn his ways. They will guide you in your life," Grandma said.

Deep inside, the boy knew he wanted to be like the grizzly bear. He didn't want to be angry with his father or afraid of anything. The grizzly would always be there to help him now. Lawrence didn't feel so alone anymore.

"Someday I'll tell Papa everything that happened when he was away at war," he said.

"You will have a lot to tell him. You have grown up since he went away."

Lawrence turned from the firelight and looked at the sky. Shafts of green light shimmered above.

"Look, Kokom. Cipayak." Lawrence pointed to the Northern Lights.

Grandma saw them too. "Our people believe the lights are the spirits of our ancestors. Your grandmothers and grandfathers are watching over you."

The Northern Lights grew brighter. Streaks of purple, red and yellow lit up the sky.

Grandma put her arm around Lawrence's shoulder. "The spirits are dancing beautifully for you tonight," she said.

As he sat by the fire, Lawrence felt the comforting presence of his ancestors.

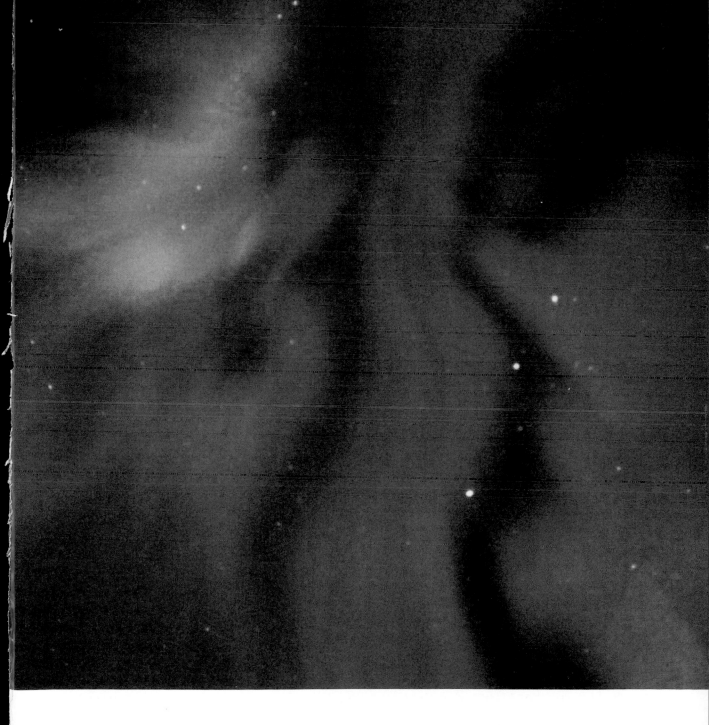

The Northern Lights (aurora borealis) looking straight up.

EPILOGUE

Papa (Victor Loyie) wearing his moss-green Canadian Armed Forces uniform, wedge-shaped cap and shiny black boots.

Lawrence (LARRY LOYIE) lived a traditional Cree life before the Second World War (1939-1945). His home was on Rabbit Hill near the town of Slave Lake in northern Alberta. Most of his family's food came from the forest, lakes and rivers. Lawrence learned from the elders, including his grandfather Edward Twin, grandmother Bella Twin and uncle Louis Twin.

The war brought many changes to young Lawrence's life. His father (Victor Loyie) had served in the First World War (1914-1918) as a young man. At the time of this story, Victor was 43 years old with nine children and could not read or write. He was called up to serve again in the Canadian Armed Forces because soldiers were needed overseas.

With Papa gone, Mama (Marie) raised the family alone. Lawrence, his older sister Elizabeth, and two younger sisters Margaret and Louise (also known as Maruk) are included in the story.

Lawrence struggles with daily chores while wrestling with the meaning of war. He misses his father's traditional teachings about their natural way of life.

With so many hunters away, natural foods like wild meat and fish were hard to get. Food now came from the store and not the land. In 1942, the Canadian government began to ration food. Whole milk was not available because it was needed for the war effort. Families drank Klim (milk spelled backward), a drink made from a powder. Unhealthy changes such as canned meats came to the diets of First Nations people.

During the Second World War, the isolated town of Slave Lake, Alberta, began to grow and change. Lawrence's family lived nearby on Rabbit Hill. They also experienced many changes to their traditional Cree lifestyle of living off the land.

With every day of the war, the world came closer to the small town of Slave Lake. Lawrence's family was one of the few to own a battery-operated radio. It made it possible for Mama to listen to war correspondents broadcasting from London, England, and other battle zones. These were some of the first radio broadcasts from war zones. The dramatic accounts "brought the war home," notes the Canadian War Museum.

War work brought strangers to the town. United States Army soldiers passed through on the train to begin construction of the Alaska Highway linking Dawson Creek, British Columbia, and Fairbanks, Alaska. The work was difficult. Ten thousand soldiers and 6,000 others hacked through muskeg and bush to complete the highway in eight months. Lawrence and Elizabeth were amazed to see the U.S. soldiers stop briefly on the railroad track, and they never saw them again.

A little known fact is that during the Second World War, more than 6,300 soldiers deserted the Canadian Armed Forces or were Away Without Leave. The police were on the alert for these "runaways" (Otapaseewuk in Cree) who harassed the communities of the north, stealing food and clothing. Lawrence's family was threatened, which brought them closer together. Lawrence showed courage when confronted by the runaways. Through his actions, he earned the respect of his elders.

First Nations men and women have always joined the armed forces in high numbers. Over time, many (like Victor Loyie) lost their status as Indians simply because they joined war efforts. After serving their country, many were denied rights and benefits equal to non-First Nations veterans. Victor returned safely to his family but never received his rightful benefits.

The author's father later in life after he returned to Alberta.

The immense contribution of First Nations, Métis and Inuit people to the security of Canada in times of war and peace is now recognized. This book was written to honour and remember all veterans, Native and non-Native.

Lawrence's story continues in the award-winning children's book As Long as the Rivers Flow (Groundwood Books).

Cree Words in the story

Kokom – Grandmother
Maruk – a frog's croak, the nickname for sister
    Louise
Mistatim – Horse
Tansi – Hello
Bannock – a kind of bread

Mosoom – Grandfather
Wihkasin – Tasty
Mah! – an exclamation
Puya – a Cree name
Kayas – "It's been a long time."
Cipayak – Northern Lights/aurora borealis

Credits and Permissions

Notes on rationing, effect of Second World War on children, and war broadcasts, courtesy of Canadian War Museum, Ottawa, Ontario

Photos of Alberta by Nelson Lutz: p 6, p 12-13, p 17, p 21, p 35, p 39

Cover photo of aurora borealis by Roman Krochuk

Photo of birch trees by Peter McFarlane: p 30

Additional images:

Mama and Papa, p 6, courtesy Larry Loyie
Louis Twin, p 8, courtesy Gladys Morrison/Nan Yuodelis
Working dogs, p 9, courtesy Gladys Morrison/Nan Yuodelis
Team of horses, p 10, courtesy La Société Historique et Généalogique de Smoky River
Lawrence Loyie, p 12, courtesy Métis Nation of Alberta and Grouard-McLennan Diocese
Elizabeth Loyie, p 12, courtesy La Société Historique et Généalogique de Smoky River
Margaret and Maruk (Louise) Loyie, p 13, courtesy La Société Historique et Généalogique de Smoky River
Main Street, p 14, courtesy Grouard Native Cultural Arts Museum
Northern Alberta Railway steam train, p 15, courtesy Alberta Railway Museum
Slave Lake school, p 17, by Joe Kirkpatrick, courtesy Slave Lake Pioneers
Ration book and stamps, p 19, courtesy Kinosayo Museum
Edward Twin, p 20, courtesy Larry Loyie
Soldiers in Dawson Creek, p 23, courtesy Alberta Railway Museum
The postmaster, p 24, courtesy Slave Lake Pioneers
Papa's war postcard, p 25, courtesy Larry Loyie
Battery-operated radio, p 26, courtesy Larry Loyie
Bella Twin, p 27, courtesy Roland Eben-Ebenau
Campsite, title page, p 29, courtesy Constance Brissenden
Birch curls and moose horn, p 33, courtesy Suzanne Bates
Blanket under spruce tree, p 33, courtesy Joel Mercer
Papa in Lawrence's dream, p 35, courtesy Larry Loyie
Cougar and grizzly bear, p 36, with permission of istockphoto
Lawrence, p 37, courtesy La Société Historique et Généalogique de Smoky River
Papa in uniform, p 40, courtesy Larry Loyie
Slave Lake, p 41, courtesy La Société Historique et Généalogique de Smoky River
Papa (Victor Loyie), p 42, courtesy Roland Eben-Ebenau
Larry Loyie, p 44, courtesy Constance Brissenden

Author Larry Loyie

Award-winning First Nations author Larry Loyie was born in Slave Lake, Alberta, where he spent his early years living a traditional Cree life. He began school in Slave Lake, but later attended St. Bernard's Mission residential school in Grouard, Alberta. After returning to school later in life, Larry received a Canada Post Literacy Award for Individual Achievement.

When the Spirits Dance is the second book in the "Lawrence Series." It begins in 1941 in northern Alberta during the Second World War. The story of Lawrence is based on the author's life, learning the traditions of his elders while experiencing a rapidly changing world. The story continues in **As Long as the Rivers Flow** (Groundwood Books), winner of the 2003 Norma Fleck Award for Canadian Children's Non-Fiction. In 2006, it was chosen as the Honour Book of the year by the First Nation Communities Read program.

Larry's third children's book, **The Gathering Tree** (Theytus Books) is a gentle introduction to HIV awareness with a First Nations storyline.

Constance Brissenden, co-author, is an award-winning freelance writer and editor. In 1993, the couple formed Living Traditions Writers Group to encourage First Nations people to write about their traditional lifestyles and history. They live in Vancouver, British Columbia, and High Prairie, Alberta. Their website is: www.firstnationswriter.com.